Christianity:

The Sad and Shameful Truth

James McQuitty

Other recent titles by James McQuitty

The Complete Guide to Spiritual Astro-Numerology

Help Yourself to a Better Life

How Psychics and Mediums Work, The Spirit and the Aura

Know Yourself

The Reason Why You Were Born

The Wisdom Oracle

Where I use the words *should* or *must* in this book it is
purely for convenience and is not intended to be a
dogmatic statement. I recognise and appreciate the
fact that we each have freewill and, ultimately, are
responsible to no one but ourselves.

www.jamesmcquitty.com

Contents

Foreword

Over recent years in the UK numerous TV programmes have been shown concerning the history of Christianity. If you have ever watched any of these revealing documentaries you will already be aware that it has a bloody, brutal, sad and shameful past.

The religions of this world have been a chain around the throats of humanity. They have caused numerous conflicts and wars, tortured, controlled and manipulated to suit their desires, making themselves into mega-rich institutions along the way. What is even worse is that they have suppressed the spread of genuine spiritual knowledge. True liberty will come only when these chains are removed.

I have no wish to undermine faith and hope, because at times this may be all we have. My intention is to present readers with factual information, to enable them to re-evaluate what they may have been taught in a new, brighter and honest light.

As for myself, I am not in any sense an 'academic' or religious scholar - so you will find that what I present in this book is easy to read and understand. Furthermore, I am being brief, otherwise the subject could fill volumes, but I believe I say enough to help readers move forward with greater, and sufficient, awareness.

Where I mention passages from the Bible I have paraphrased and amended them so that they are easier to read in our present day language.

Chapter One

From Nature Worship to Christianity

For a great many years ancient humankind's observations of nature - the vegetation (ecological) and the weather (meteorological) - and later the sun and stars (astronomical), was at times far from the modern perspective of scientific.

Their speculations were influenced by superstitions and fearful instincts, which led them to believe in a kind of magic, and in the existence of unseen gods of nature.

Their fears led to the development of taboos, traditions, and rituals around which ceremony often developed, and then to tribal and eventually national laws. Such practices were in effect the earliest forms of religion and the forerunners to modern-day religion.

Festivals were held to celebrate various aspects of nature, including those for the changing seasons. They recognised the annual decrease and increase of the power of the sun — its seeming death, and rebirth, with the rebirth of vegetation. In time this was transformed to become the death and resurrection of the men who were later proclaimed as "saviours" and "Gods" upon earth.

At one time the Earth herself (the feminine is used for convenience) was viewed as the fertile Mother of all things. She had temples and alters erected and dedicated to her in the majority of the cities of ancient Greece; and was known as the goddess Gaia. She was considered mother and mate of Uranus (the sky), the mother of the seas, mountains, and all the natural features of the world.

Some of the Gods, such as Helios (the sun), were considered friendly, while others were believed bad, unhappy or cruel.

When a good harvest was forthcoming, and the weather fine, the people assumed they were pleasing to the Gods. When severe storms, gales, and floods came, and worse when earthquakes and volcanic occurred, bringing fear, the people believed that bad or unhappy Gods were in control. Thunder was considered to be the voice of an angry God and lightning strikes a punishment.

People reasoned that if a God saw fit to punish, then someone or something must be displeasing them. Consequently, because they lacked understanding of the natural workings of nature, they developed the idea that the Gods, just like themselves, would like gifts, offerings, and ultimately sacrifices made to them.

Some went as far as offering members of their own tribe through sacrifice; someone with virtue or high standing was considered the greatest offering. The greater the sacrifices made, the more the people reasoned the Gods would reward them, or free them from the destruction of nature. Child sacrifice was not uncommon and many remains have been uncovered by archaeologists. The Old Testament of the Bible actually mentions such sacrifices – including 'their sons and their daughters.' (Psalms)

In ancient times around the globe, including in Africa, Australia, Egypt, Fiji, Mexico and Tahiti to name just a few, many people practiced cannibalism – and even this has been carried forward into Christianity.

Human sacrifice and cannibalism continued in many areas until much more recent times, and the famous explorer Captain Cook even witnessed the practice of sacrifice in Tahiti as recently as 1777. The local Chief had ordered a man to be sacrificed (killed) to seek the aid of the 'great god in the war.'

The eating of sacrificed victims is what numerous religions, such as those of Babylon, Egypt, Greece and Mexico and eventually the Christian religion based the Eucharist ceremony on. In the modern Christian ceremony, the eating of bread and wine symbolically represents the body and blood of Jesus, the Christ. The word Christ came from Greek, meaning the "anointed one," as the chosen one was anointed, or covered with oil, prior to becoming the sacrificed victim, to enhance the taste of the flesh to be cooked and eaten.

In regard to the Christian (Catholic) Eucharist ceremony, Pope Innocent III (1215) decreed that the wafer they eat and the wine they drink during this ceremony did not "represent" the body and blood of Jesus; it (magically) "became" his body and blood, and this is still the official interpretation of what would (if it were true) be an act of cannibalism.

What has been described as "Ancestral worship" was also practiced in ancient times. Amongst ancient people and throughout history there have always been those who have had mediumistic gifts. The natural mediums of the tribes were able to see and report the sightings of those tribe members who had passed on. Others too may have seen them, just as many people today see what they would call a spirit or ghost.

A sighting of a former tribe member would have been received with awe, and any guidance received through such a communication would have been considered a great blessing, as the returning spirit was considered to be residing with the Gods. (Then, even as today, many people were ignorant of the fact that everyone survives death). Each returning ancestor also took on the role of a separate God, and their advice and direction were given great reverence by the mostly obedient people. The early forerunner to the priesthood embraced and welcomed such communications.

Over time (I am skimming through history) human weakness led to some of the early priests becoming corrupt. They realised that with a little trickery they could quite easily fool the simple people of those ancient times, and so profit for themselves.

Hidden devices for the creation of illusions have been found in some ancient temples, such as equipment for the raising of a platform, to evoke the appearance of levitation. Tubes have also been found, which enabled a hidden priest to answer questions while the answer appeared to come directly from a carved figure revered by the people. The carved figure had an opening so that payment could be taken for the advice or answer given. (The Church has always been pleased to take money).

Over the passage of time the ancient priesthood gained in power, and easily fooled and dominated people, and when they deemed it necessary, discredited or condemned the genuine mediums.

Until the fourth century, when they were denounced as evil by the Christian Church, the Jewish Apostolic Church held services akin to modern day Spiritualism, where the medium took the lead role, with spirit world communications and such practices as trance communication being the accepted norm. This fact is recorded in the preserved writings of one of Rome's most renowned jurists, a man named Tertullian who lived from 160-230.

Mediumship, with its potential for spirit world communications of truth, obviously did not suit the corrupt priesthood, as this would have denied them the positions of power and authority which they made so lucrative for themselves.

Gradually the very people they imitated, the true mediums, were disposed of by ridicule, or by laws introduced by the priesthood. Thus they took control and directed life, taking a share of income through offerings demanded (supposedly) in the name of God.

The early priesthood also claimed that all forms of ill-health were a punishment from God, and that only they, as chosen intermediaries of God, could heal. But if the sick failed to recover, as was oft the case, priest's said it was because the sufferer was in some way undeserving, or because they lacked sufficient faith. The priesthood obviously could not lose; they could get credit one way, but no blame the other. Later in this book you will read how the Christian Church was still claiming as much in the middle of the twentieth century.

Certainly not all priests throughout history have been party to trickery and illusion to promote their teaching. This was unnecessary because the early Christian Church instructed future priests with the teachings they formulated, and forbid other learning. By doing so they ensured that new priests could have no knowledge other than which they were permitted to learn. All knowledge deemed undesirable was denounced as evil and the work of the devil, and to seek such was deemed sinful.

Some ancient people, and in particular the early priesthood, came to the conclusion that only those with God-like powers, and the authority of God, could return to communicate and help direct the lives of those on earth. With a little logical reasoning by the priesthood, it soon became just a small step for them to reach the conclusion that if one who returned after death was a God-man, or a son of God, then that same man must have been so when they were on earth.

Myths and legends undoubtedly sprang up about such men. With only word of mouth, and with no books or modern methods of recording details, exaggeration was in all probability rife. With the passage of time such legends became established as saviours, and sons of God.

As different phases of belief overlapped it was only natural to bestow upon the newly 'elected' sons of God the legends and beliefs of the old. So old beliefs were absorbed within the new to make it far easier to appease or convert people. Therefore the sacrifice of the martyr, the tribe member who gave his life for the benefit of the rest of the tribe, was connected to the new legend, ultimately becoming the sacrifice so all could live eternally in heaven with the martyred son and his father God.

All of course relates back to nature worship – the sacrifice of the harvested crops – and their resurrection (re-growth) in spring as they returned from seeming death.

This historical "saviour-God" syndrome occurred on numerous occasions throughout history, and the legends that teach of such God-men probably reached every culture throughout the world. Known religious and historical records shown in books such as "The Rock of Truth" by Arthur Findlay list sixteen such saviour-Gods before Christianity elevated Jesus to the same level at the council of Nicaea in the year 325.

While in "Faiths, Facts, and Frauds of Religious History" by Emma Hardinge Britten, the author lists thirty four Avatars or God-men, and also mentions a book by Mr. K. Graves, an American, under the title of "Sixteen Crucified Saviours."

All the so-called saviour-Gods had a common theme. Namely that each of the saviours were said to have be born of virgin mothers, in a cave, barn, stable, shed or similar, to have been attended by wise men who came with gifts, who themselves had been informed of the intended birth by God's angels. Each child was said to have amazed their elders with wisdom beyond the possibilities of their upbringing, and was reported to have later preached peace and love, yet ultimately become the victim of their enemies through persecution, followed by a mock trial and execution. After each execution, great storms, earthquakes or darkness descended. Within a few days, the saviour-God was reported to be risen from the dead, providing proof of their continued life.

Later, (and in the case of Christianity 325 years later), the saviour was proclaimed the son of God, who came into physical incarnation to pave the way for mere mortals' entry into heaven.

One of the saviour-Gods, Krishna, like the young Jesus, had to flee with his parents from a tyrant king who sought his death. Krishna reportedly was taken to the town of Mathura, the same town that in an early gospel manuscript Jesus was reportedly taken to when his life was in similar danger.

Another interesting comparison can be made, and authenticated, with the saviour-God Bel. Because an ancient tablet which still exists today in the British Museum in London relates a passion play of his life story, and this is nearly identical to the reported life story of Jesus.

Throughout history there have been many men who were elevated to the level of a God, but only those believed to have come to earth to die as a supreme sacrifice for the benefit of others, became considered a "saviour-God." Those historically recorded as such, with approximate dates in chronological order, were:

1.   Osiris, Egypt, 1700 BC

2.   Bel, Babylon, 1200 BC

3.   Atys, Phrygia, 1170 BC

4.   Thammuz, Syria, 1160 BC

5.   Dionysus, Greece, 1100 BC

6.   Krishna, India, 1000 BC

7.   Hesus, Europe, 834 BC

8.   Indra, Thibet, 725 BC

9.   Bali, Asia, 725 BC

10. Iao, Nepaul, 622 BC

11. Alcestis, Pherac, 600 BC

12. Quexalcote, Mexico, 587 BC

13. Wittoba, Travancore, 552 BC

14. Prometheus, Greece, 547 BC

15. Quirinus, Rome, 506 BC

16. Mithra, Persia, 400 BC

What matters most is not the number of God-men or saviour-Gods, but the similarity of their recorded life stories. I believe that the information contained within this chapter is well known to those in positions of authority within the Christian Church, but sadly they do not present it to their congregations.

In Britain, as long ago as 1933, Arthur Findlay, who amongst other achievements in life was a renowned religious historian, challenged all the Protestant parsons in Great Britain, at the time some 28,630 of them, to answer his book "The Rock of Truth," but none responded. The Church prefers to keep their followers ignorant of such historical fact, continuing as they have done for nearly seventeen hundred years.

By the fourth century the orthodox priesthood was well established throughout the Roman Empire where since approximately 70 BC the religion of Mithraism was practiced. At one time, Mithraism was the most widespread religion of the Western world, having crossed much of Europe from its original home in Persia where it was established around 400 BC.

The saviour-God Mithra, who was also considered a sun-God, had reportedly experienced a similar life and death story as Christians teach about Jesus. The birthday of Mithra, December 25th, was a celebrated festival, as was the spring equinox, now known to us as Easter, which comes from the name Eostre, who was the Anglo-Saxon Goddess of spring. This was the time of year when Mithra was said to have been executed and to have risen from his tomb. The actual day of the rising was a Sunday, and because of this it was referred to as "The Lords Day."

An earlier meaning for Sunday was copied by the Jewish people from the Babylonian word Sabatu, meaning Sabbath. This was the day when God was believed to have rested after the creation of the world. Additionally, the decision to give the copied birthday of December 25th to Jesus was not decided upon by monks, and decreed so by the Emperor, until the year 527. Also, the symbolic image of Jesus on a cross did not appear until the year 680, when it was decreed by the Emperor that this should replace the Mithraic symbol of a lamb on the cross. The Lamb represented the people's sins being taken away through sacrifice.

In ancient times a ceremony, a baptism of blood from a slaughtered lamb was performed, when the one being confirmed (an adult who confirms their acceptance of faith in their religion) stood below a grated alter, while the priest above killed a lamb and allowed its blood to pour through to the initiate below. Today its modern counterpart is the Christian ceremony of Atonement or Confirmation, which is also supposed to represent the cancelling of sin. (Let me assure you, nobody escapes natural spiritual justice).

But it is quite likely the image of the Lamb has much greater historical meaning, for in section II of "Faiths, Facts, and Frauds of Religious History" by Emma Hardinge Britten, the author mentions the astrological studies of races who lived seven to eight thousand years ago in such places as Egypt and India, where the position of the sun in the "heavens" and the constellations of stars had already been divided into twelve groups or signs of the zodiac, complete with names such as the Bull, Lion and Ram.

All the God-men or saviour-God's who were expected to come to earth periodically, like Mithra, were also considered sun-Gods. One who arrived during the sign of the Bull would have been represented on earth by the image of the Bull, while one who arrived during the sign of the Ram — or Lamb as it became — was represented by this image.

Even the celebrated "Lord's Prayer," which is an old Jewish prayer - and we must remember that

Jesus was himself Jewish, was copied by the Jewish people from the Babylonians, as an ancient clay tablet discovered in 1882 bearing the same sentiments revealed.

We can see how each old belief or idea is carried over to the new in order to appease those who dislike the change. Even the religion of Mithraism did likewise, for long before saviour-Gods, December 25th was celebrated by sun worshippers as the Solstice (21st really) or the beginning of winter, after which date the days lengthen and the sun gradually strengthens. Similarly, Easter developed from the celebration of the spring equinox — the beginning of spring, and the return to life, or resurrection, of growth. The new growth saved the people from starvation; hence all saviours, such as Jesus and Mithra, were said to have risen at this particular time of year.

Along with copying the life story of Mithra and all the festivals and ceremonies of that religion, even the Christian churches were built to face east, just as the older churches of Mithraism did. No doubt the religion of Mithra had themselves copied its predecessor and so forth back along the chain to the practices of sun worshippers, east being the direction of the rising sun.

The word "Amen," the now traditional method of closing a prayer, these days considered to mean "so be it," comes from the Egyptian Sun God "Amen" or "Ra-Amen." The Egyptians closed their prayers by saying something along the lines of: "Thank you, Amen." This method of closing a prayer was then copied by enslaved Jewish people, and later by Christians.

I believe the true life story of Jesus to be a reasonably normal one. It is likely that he either joined the Jewish sect known as the Essenes or became influenced by their teachings. But the Essenes would not have known him by the name of Jesus, which is a Greek translation of his name; in the Jewish language he would have been known as Jeshuah.

The Essenes were one of three major Jewish sects during the lifetime of Jesus, and their teachings were the basis of everything Jesus reportedly taught. They also practiced the art of spiritual healing, and very likely trained Jesus in this form of mediumship. The Essenes were believed to have been an offshoot of Buddhism, following the teachings of the Buddha which spread from India.

The Essenes encouraged a life of service, and to strive for purity, and lived an almost monastic life. It was considered a virtue to give to the poor, and to seek no personal treasures upon earth, believing their reward would come in heaven. They had no set leaders, and believed in total equality.

The Essene teachers were not welcomed by the leaders of the more orthodox Jewish religion. When Jesus began to teach and heal, he too became a victim of their criticism. The Bible tells of an incident when Jesus was in danger of execution 'for blasphemy' some time before the crucifixion. (John)

Jewish records of the second century say Jesus was tried and condemned in a Jewish court before being stoned and hanged, and certainly 'they took him down from the tree' is recorded in the Bible (Acts)

Within a few years of the passing of Jesus, Paul, or Saul as he was previously known, who was not a disciple of Jesus, and had actually never met him in physical life, had an experience, a "visitation," on the road to Damascus, which he described as "a light from heaven." (Acts)

He also said he heard a voice and believed it to be a communication from Jesus, asking him why he was 'persecuting' him. (Acts)

Paul, who was born around the same time as Jesus, and is believed to have passed around the year 65, had until this time, as a Rabbi with the authority of the Jewish priesthood, persecuted the "Jesuians," as the early followers of Jesus or his teachings were known. He freely admits causing these people imprisonment and death. (Acts) In fact, Paul was on the way to Damascus for the purpose of making further arrests.

Paul was familiar with the teachings and beliefs surrounding the Greek saviour-God Dionysus, who was the God of Paul's home town, Tarsus, (in present day Turkey and in Paul's time a cosmopolitan university city on the main trade route between East and West). These included the belief that a messiah would one day come to earth, in this case the reincarnation of Dionysus.

As a result of the visitation, it is highly likely that Paul believed Jesus to be the fulfilment of this ancient prophecy. It was a common belief in those days that such a visitation as Paul claims was possible only if coming from a God – a carryover from Ancestral worship.

The belief in a second coming is in fact an ancient idea, and can be traced back to sun worship, when the sun-God was awaited each morning with prayer and thanksgiving. The Jews of Paul's time were also expecting God to send a Messiah — some looked for a supernatural being who would establish righteousness and justice, while others expected a military leader who would drive out the Romans.

When one looks at what Paul had been taught about Dionysus, namely that he was born of a virgin impregnated by Zeus, that he suffered and died for humankind, and was a divine creation who humbled himself to save humanity, it comes as no surprise to find he then taught almost exactly the same about Jesus.

Gradually the saviour-God syndrome was once again established around a new figure. Paul spent the remainder of his life travelling and preaching his new found belief and finding converts to the new religion of Christianity.

In those days Rome was the home of the most powerful rulers in existence. Rome, and the West of the Roman Empire in the years 312-337 (the entire empire from 324), was ruled by the emperor who became known as Constantine the Great. Constantine was a fairly liberal emperor, as emperors went in those days, even though he did murder his wife, eldest son, nephew and numerous others. But that was acceptable then, as the emperor ruled supreme. In fact, until Constantine declined the title, all emperors before him had been considered Emperor-Gods, so the concept of God-men, as with Mithra and then Jesus, was perfectly acceptable to the people.

Constantine took a liking to Christianity, and despite never being a full Christian himself, in due course decreed that it was to be the new state religion of the Roman Empire.

Why he chose to make this change is possibly due to the fact that Christianity had, by this time, spread into every land ruled by Rome, whereas Mithraism was less widespread, and Constantine wanted to unite the empire, which was in danger of decentralisation into independent states. Constantine believed that under one religion, people would feel more united, and thus give strength to the empire.

The powerful bishops of that period of early Christian supremacy still could not agree on the 'divinity' of Jesus. Some of them taught he was a mortal who brought forth the word of God, and others taught he was a God who lived among men.

To settle the disagreement between the various bishops of the early Christian Church, Constantine ordered a council to agree a common teaching. This was the reason for the now infamous council at Nicaea in 325, which was to shape the new state religion of Christianity.

Although during the council the bishops still argued for and against the divinity of Jesus, Constantine forced the issue, and demanded a majority vote. Those in favour of Jesus being elevated to the status of a saviour-God won the day, and so it has been taught by Christians ever since.

Once Jesus had been proclaimed the 'son of God,' a royal command was issued stating that everyone had to believe in the new teaching. Those people, including some bishops, who opposed it, were cast out as heretics, while those who supported it gained promotion to higher positions within the Church.

When considering the decision of the council at Nicaea, one can easily imagine the pressure the bishops were under to at least elevate Jesus to an equal standing with Mithra, in order to satisfy the people as to his worth, and therefore the worth and standing of the bishops and the Church itself.

The new state religion most certainly did not please all of the followers of Mithraism, but since those who objected to the ruling of Constantine could quite legally be killed without any fear or threat of prosecution, the majority were forced to go along with the change.

The collation of manuscripts to form the earliest Christian Bible during the late 4th century, copying the Buddhist concept, was simply the basis for the New Testament, and it was the sixth century before it was combined with the Old Testament to produce the first complete Bible, an early forerunner of today's version.

This original form would have differed considerably from the present day Bible, as over the centuries certain manuscripts were added and others omitted so as to favour those in authority. It was not until as late as the year 1611 that version's similar to the present day ones were produced. (The Catholic and Protestant Bibles differ in the number of books included from 73 to 66). By the time the current editions were printed it was impossible to be sure how many original writings remained, as the manuscripts were rewritten time and again by numerous monks and priests.

The latter chapters of Mark were certainly additions to justify torture and murder, for they damn all who had not been baptized and did not believe, and are not to be found in the oldest remaining copies of manuscripts.

A later revision of the Bible was undertaken in 1881, and those who carried out this revision stated they had discovered more than thirty-six thousand mistakes, which really does emphasis the absurdity of claiming the Bible to be the irrefutable word of God – as sadly some still do.

The early Christian bishops set about their task of ruling the ignorant masses by ensuring they remained ignorant, by their closure of schools, and teaching that to seek unnecessary knowledge, other than the teaching of Christianity, was disrespectful of God, and akin to evil. They added that those who did not believe in Jesus would suffer eternal torment in hell. (What shameful lies).

These teachings were a far cry from the days prior to Christianity, when those Christians refer to as Pagans taught that God was the Father of all, and that each person was to be considered as a son or daughter of God.

In the year 410 Rome was overrun by the Visigoths, leaving the Roman Empire without civil command. At this time the Christian Church, with its first Pope, took control of the Empire and its 120 million people.

Despite splits, such as the Reformation of the sixteenth century, when those who have become known as Protestants split from the Catholic faith, and all the other sects or branches of Christianity which have since splintered away, the original teaching that Jesus was the only true son of God remains the mainstay teaching of Christianity, a teaching based upon zero factual evidence, and a fictional tale based on nature worship.

I wonder how many people, if from childhood had been taught the true origins of institutional Christianity as briefly outlined herein, would still choose to follow the Christian faith?

Chapter Two

Bible Contradictions and Fantasy

Christians often refer to the Bible as "the good book" and "the word of God," yet to anyone studying it without the prejudiced indoctrination of a Christian upbringing such descriptions would most certainly never come to mind.

The Bible is clearly a collection of man written words, prejudiced by the times and circumstances which prevailed when they were written, full of contradiction and nonsense. It makes liberal use of the name of God, often in association with murder, war, revenge and destruction, while in other chapters and verses it claims the love of God is for all.

Within its pages it states one of the so called commandments of God as given to Moses: 'you must not kill' (Exodus and Deuteronomy)

While elsewhere it states how God instructed Moses 'to avenge the children of Israel' (Numbers) and how after a battle, had thousands of captured men, women and children killed. The male prisoners went first, and as though this was not bad enough, they then went ahead and killed all the boys and all the women who were 'not virgins.' Yet, according to the Bible, they were permitted to keep the virgin women as their wives, some thirty-two thousand of them.

These days, even in circumstances of war, it would be called kidnap and rape, and a long prison sentence would follow for such war crimes.

If this account of the laws of Moses, and therefore supposedly of God, are not ridiculously insulting enough to the true God of love, how about this:

'If a man has a stubborn and rebellious son who will not obey his father or mother' the Bible instructs that they should be stoned to death, and that 'everyone should hear of this and fear.' (Deuteronomy)

If any Christian today is truly gullible enough to totally accept Bible teachings, they should ask themselves why the laws of Christian countries do not reflect what it says. The answer is because any person with an ounce of commonsense, reason or fair judgment realises that the Bible does not reflect the total truth of history, or of how life should be led, no more than it reflects the true laws or teachings of God.

The story of Noah's ark, as told by Moses in Genesis, is a fantasy that totally lacks commonsense.

In this crazy fictitious story God (supposedly) saw that the wickedness of people on earth had grown so great with every thought evil that he said, 'I will destroy man (and women and animals etc) whom I have created from the face of the earth.' But (somehow) Noah 'found grace in the eyes of the Lord (God).'

According to the Bible, God then proceeded to instruct Noah to build an ark, and gave instructions as to its material and size, telling Noah that he and his wife, three sons, and their wives, and two of every living thing, along with adequate provisions, should be taken on board the ark. Although in later instructions, at the start of chapter seven, some, such as fowls, were increased in numbers to seven. Are we to assume God made a mistake in his original instructions?

During the floods which reportedly followed, Noah reached six hundred years of age. After some one hundred and fifty days afloat, all life upon earth other than in the ark was destroyed.

At the end of the story, when the land was dry, and all had disembarked from the ark, we are told that God then instructed Noah and his sons to begin repopulating the earth. 'God blessed Noah and his sons,' and said, 'be fruitful, and multiply, and replenish the earth.'

This is obviously stating that God encouraged a vast amount of very close breeding, and perhaps even incest, to replenish the earth. In the same manner incest would have been the only way the human race could have got started if we were to believe in the Bible story of Adam and Eve, as told in Genesis. How very unpleasant the thought is.

The story continues by saying that the sons of Noah disembarked from the ark 'and of them was the whole earth repopulated.'

It also says that after the flood Noah lived another three-hundred-and-fifty years, and did not pass until he was nine-hundred-and-fifty years old.

If Christians are sad and gullible enough to believe that the story of Noah's ark is a true one, this story teaches that God destroyed all men, women, children, newly born babies, pregnant mothers to be, the old and infirm, the blind, and the crippled and practically every innocent animal.

I ask, does this really sound like a just and forgiving God, one who also tells us to love our enemies? The whole episode, as with so much of the Bible, is full of contradiction, fabrication and fantasy in an attempt to favour those who wished to dominate others. It is an example of how the Bible has and is sometimes still used to keep Christians in fear of a revengeful and cruel God.

Another point Christians are unable to answer concerns the age of Noah. If we were to believe the Bible, we would have to accept the amazing longevity of Noah. Why did he live so long? And did he have other wives whom he outlived before the one at the time of the flood? Then, we might ask, what about all the years between his reported age of six hundred at the time of the flood and his passing at the age of nine hundred and fifty years. Did his wife live to be as old as he? Then what are we to make of his three sons and their wives. Were the sons the product of Noah's most recent marriage at the time of the flood, and did he have other families whom he had outlived? Did he ignore and leave to drown all the grandchildren and great grandchildren from previous marriages? Or are we to assume that Noah waited until he was well into his five-hundreds before he married and had his only three sons? Or were the three sons and their wives also hundreds of years old? Surely this would have made the repopulating of the world a tiring, if not biologically impossible task for them all?

One can only guess at the thinking and reasoning processes of the millions of Christians who blindly accept this story when it presents such fictitious and unbelievable stories as fact; for a story it obviously is, and one which, like all Christian teachings, is not truly unique.

In "Faiths, Facts, and Frauds of Religious History" by Emma Hardinge Britten, the author relates how ancient Astrology was the basis for all the flood stories. The water sign of Aquarius played a vital part in such legends, and it depended upon which star sign was predominant at any particular astronomical cycle, as to whether the belief that destruction by flood or fire was imminent.

The accounts so far mentioned from the Old Testament are so very contradictory to the teachings attributed to Jesus in the Bible, whom Christians regard as a one third aspect of God, and therefore equal creator of all life. The following Bible teachings show Jesus, thus God, in a completely different light to the God who Moses would have us fear:

'You have heard it said that you should love thy neighbour, and hate your enemy. But I (Jesus) say, love your enemies, bless them that curse you, do good to them that hate you, and pray for others.' (Matthew)

Christian ministers sometimes quote from the Bible to condemn any form of mediumship, and regard the practices of Spiritualist churches as occult evil. They quote passages which condemn mediums and ignore those which favour and encourage practices which can only be labelled mediumistic. Christian ministers also seem to either ignore, or justify, the savagery, brutality and cruelty that went on supposedly with the approval of God.

The following are typical examples of Biblical extracts used by Christian ministers to create fear, and to discredit mediumship and Spiritualism.

'You should not allow a witch (meaning a medium or a healer) to live.' (Exodus)

'You should not use divination, or consult with familiar spirits, or a wizard, because these things are an abomination.' (Deuteronomy)

'Saul died because of the transgression he committed by seeking counsel of one that had a 'familiar spirit' – a medium. Therefore God killed him and gave the Kingdom to David.' (1 Chronicles)

Those considered evil by Christian Bible teachings include astrologers, charmers, diviners or soothsayers (those who seek to foresee the future), dreamers, enchanters, idolaters, murderers and liars, those who use a familiar spirit, (otherwise known as a medium, necromancer, witch, wizard, or sorcerer), observers of times, prophets, (though apparently only the "false" prophets who did not teach the Christian party-line, those who did were considered to be teaching under direct inspiration from God), plus those who pass through fire (whatever they are), whoremongers, and the unbelieving.

I can add to this list some other contemporary practices listed by Christian ministers as divination, and therefore in their teaching occult and evil, such as card or tarot card reading, palmistry, dowsing, and even the reading of a horoscope.

If we were silly enough to take the Bible and the teaching of Christian ministers at their word, millions of people throughout the world are involving themselves with occult practices, and are thereby doing evil, and as such, according to their teaching, should be seeking the 'ministry of deliverance.' What does this entail? Typical Christian teaching from handouts commonly available suggests those involved should 'stop the activity, repent involvement in occultism, and ask Jesus for forgiveness,' for they say 'the cross of Jesus was the place of victory over sin, death and evil, and his blood will cleanse you from all of Satan's residual rubbish.' (The magical transformation of wine into blood gets another mention).

Rubbish is also the first word which springs to my mind when I read this, for if they consider anyone who reads their horoscope as involving themselves with evil, they are truly living in the past, along with the source and basis for their beliefs.

There are passages in the Bible which give a completely different outlook to the Christian teaching of fear and punishment by God for those who practice, or have dealings with, what they classify as occult. This includes all those who simply use their God given spiritual gifts, such as clairvoyance, clairaudience, and healing, for the benefit of others.

These say, 'concerning spiritual gifts, I would not have you ignorant. There are diversities of gifts, but the same Spirit. The manifestation of the Spirit is given to everyone, some are given knowledge and words of wisdom; others the gifts of healing, or the workings of miracles; to another prophecy;' and so forth. (1 Corinthians)

'Do not believe every spirit, but try them, whether they are of God: because many false prophets are in the world.' (1 John)

'He spoke of his holy prophets, which have been since the world began.' (Luke)

'Quench not the Spirit and do not despise prophesying. Prove all things and hold fast to that which is good.' (1 Thessalonians)

'Do not neglect the gift that is in you, which was given by prophecy, with the laying on of hands. Meditate upon these things; give yourself wholly to them.' (1 Timothy)

'Heal the sick, cleanse the lepers, raise the dead, cast out devils, what you have freely received, freely give.' (Matthew)

These examples show that parts of the Bible approve of the use and practice of spiritual gifts such as mediumship. These clearly show that the Bible manages to contradict itself on numerous occasions. It also proves that mediumship was practiced by those with a "familiar spirit," as the Bible refers to them.

As mentioned, parts of the Bible encourage healing, or the laying on of hands. Additionally it clearly states there are diversities of spiritual gifts, and include the teaching of knowledge and wisdom, perhaps by those they classify as apostles with faith. Then there are those who work miracles, and those who dream, which may refer to those who have precognitive dreams, as well as others who see visions. Some are to be prophets, as it states there have always been such. It also states that those who use their gift, should have to prove it, and that we should test the spirits, in other words, make sure the medium is genuine by the proof of the communications they receive, for false prophets, those who use trickery for their own benefit — such as the early priesthood — have always existed.

The teaching that a spiritual gift should be freely used and not neglected is a far cry from the Christian emphasis upon faith, and their teaching that seeking knowledge through spiritual communication can only lead to contact with evil spirits. How contradictory it is to say that good is stronger than evil, while at the same time saying only evil can be reached. This is not to say that those we may consider evil spirits do not exist, for they do, but they are merely the same evil spirits who once walked the earth as evil people (the torturers of the inquisition spring to mind). They hold no special power over mediums or any other person upon earth.

Continuing with contradictions from within the Bible, in one book it clearly states no man has seen God, while in another it states Moses did just that.

'No man has seen God at any time.' (St. John)

'The Lord (God) spoke to Moses face to face, as a man (or women) speaks to his friend.' (Exodus)

But then surely if Jesus was effectively God on earth all who saw him would have seen God?

Christian ministers teach that Jesus was the son of God, and not the natural son of Joseph or any other man. But this is not the case according to certain verses of the Bible, where he is reportedly the son or seed of David.

'Jesus was made of the seed of David.' (Romans and St. John)

'Jesus, the son of David, the son of Abraham.' (Matthew)

To further confuse all who study the Bible, in Matthew and in Luke the genealogy, in other words the ancestral family tree, of Jesus is reported. One would expect to find agreement here, but all we find is more contradiction, for they list a different amount of generations between David and Jesus, and with many different ancestral names quoted. Besides which, surely if Jesus was who they claim, namely the "son of God," artificially inseminated within the physical body of Mary by the Holy Ghost aspect of God, Jesus should not have a male side to his family tree, for they would have played no part in his creation.

The only family tree which might be of interest, if you were sad enough to accept any of the reports as accurate, would be that of Mary and her Mother and Grandmother and so forth back. This would be of special interest to Roman Catholics, since they accept Mary as herself being the result of an immaculate conception. They conclude that one who gives birth to an immaculate child must herself be the result of an immaculate conception. Therefore, Catholic Christians would have to accept that from the very beginning of time, the female ancestors of Mary must have all been conceived immaculately. (To take the absurdity further, we could then trace the line of Mary back to Adam and Eve and ask whether, after starting the immaculate line of Mary, Eve had other children who weren't immaculate).

Christian ministers also teach that Jesus was crucified, while some verses of the Bible state he was hanged on and later taken down from a tree.

(Acts, and 1 Peter)

There is also at least one verse in the Bible which states Jesus was crucified in Egypt. (Revelation)

Christian ministers teach that the body of Jesus, after his crucifixion, was placed in a rock tomb, but the Bible also says that he was buried. (1 Corinthians)

Christian ministers teach that communication with departed souls, or spirits, is not possible, or, that if it does occur, the communicators must be evil spirits. But what about the following verses, which confirm the return after death of Moses and Elias, who talked to Jesus and were seen by Peter and other disciples.

'There talked with him (Jesus) two men, Moses and Elias:' (Luke)

'Peter and those with him were sleeping and when they woke they saw the two men that stood with him (Jesus).' (Luke)

Another point which makes a mockery of the Christian teaching that only baptized Christians can enter heaven, is the fact Moses and Elias, like Jesus, were Jewish.

What then of the divinity of Jesus, as taught through Christianity, namely that he was the only son of God, and as such, is part of a trinity, God the Father, God the Son, and God the Holy Ghost, which is really one being. Well this supposed fact also lacks in conviction, when certain verses are considered, as they confirm he was a normal man, who taught the word of God. Furthermore, in verses from St. John and Matthew, Jesus personally confirms that which he calls the "Holy Ghost" as separate from himself, and that God, the Father, is greater than he.

'Jesus of Nazareth, a man approved of God among you by miracles and wonders and signs.' (Acts)

'I go to the Father, who is greater than I.' (St. John)

'There is none good but God.' (Matthew)

Confirmation that Jesus was a 'man of God' and a spiritual teacher, and not a one third aspect of God, can be gathered. Because surely if Jesus was who Christians claim, a one third aspect of God, would he really have asked the other two thirds why they had forsaken him? (Mark)

The very foundation of the Christian religion is built upon faith, and the Bible seems to suggest that Jesus tested the faith of his disciples by asking them to take poison. 'They (the original disciples) will take up serpents; and if they drink any deadly thing, it will not hurt them; they will lay hands on the sick, and they will recover.' (Mark)

I will leave it to Christians to decide if Jesus was suggesting his disciples should take poison purely as a test of their faith, or additionally to enhance their healing potency?

The Bible was so clearly written by men (women never got a look in) with self interest at heart, that to call it the word of God is an insult. In the following it becomes clear that God was supposedly only interested in the Jewish people, and that the writers would stop at no absurdity, even to the point of relating how God caused his creation to come to a standstill, to help their success in battle.

'The sun stood still, and the moon, until the people had avenged themselves upon their enemies. It did not to go down for a whole day. There was no day like that before or after, for the Lord (God) fought for Israel.' (Joshua)

One can only marvel at the imagination and invention of the Jewish writers who, unbeknown to themselves, were to fool millions of future Christians. If the sun and moon 'magically' stood still, and therefore the earth too, since it orbits the sun, this would cause the destruction of the entire planet as we know it. And if this was a miracle performed by God, as Christians might claim, why was the occasion not recorded anywhere else upon the planet? Surely someone, somewhere, would have noticed and recorded the miraculous occurrence, lasting as it reportedly did for a full day?

I continue with Bible verses that have been used to bring misery to countless thousands of people the world over by providing moral encouragement for slavery and the slave trade for hundreds of years. It was finally abolished and made illegal in the UK in 1833 and in the USA in 1865.

'Bondmen and bondmaids you will have of the heathen. You can also buy the children of the strangers and their families and they will be your possessions. Take them also as an inheritance for your children after you, to inherit them as a possession. They will be your bondmen forever.' (Leviticus)

Yet the contradiction with the following was completely ignored by Christians, who throughout the history of the Bible have selected the passages which favoured their needs at any given time.

'There is neither Jew nor Greek, bond or free, male or female, for you are all one in Christ Jesus.' (Galatians)

Having read all are one, and therefore presumably equal, what does the Bible say about the equality of women?

'The husband is the head of the wife, even as Christ is the head of the Church. Therefore as the Church is subject unto Christ, let the wives be to their own husbands in everything.' (Ephesians)

'Let women learn in silence with all subjection. I suffer not a woman to teach, or to usurp authority over the man, but to be in silence.' (1 Timothy)

'Let women keep silence in the churches for they are not permitted to speak. They are commanded to be under obedience. If they will learn anything, let them ask their husbands at home, for it is a shame for women to speak in the church.' (1 Corinthians)

Such was (or is) the fate of women under the directive of the Christian Bible. They are to remain in silent ignorance, or learn from their husbands at home. If they are not married, they are really in trouble.

In Christian Britain women were so poorly treated that it was even common practice for a man to take his wife to market with a halter round her neck and sell her. The last of such case was recorded as recently as 1852.

Practicing homosexuals were treated even worse than women by the Church. According to the Bible, in Leviticus, 'If a man lies with another man as those who lie with a woman, both of them have committed a detestable act, and should be put to death.'

Because of the Christian Church same sex relationships in England were not decriminalised until 1967.

One verse from the Bible does manage to correctly describe our true spiritual nature, a verse rarely quoted by Christian ministers, for it comes too close to confirming the Spiritualist teaching of continuous life with a spiritual body.

'There is a natural body (physical), and there is a spiritual body.' (1 Corinthians)

I think I have said enough about the contents of the Bible to convince any fair minded and free-thinking person that to place any trust in its accuracy, and therefore worth, would be very unwise. It is most certainly not the word of God or inspired by God, with the majority of it simply being a reflection of the times when it was written, with all the prejudice, superstition, ignorance, barbaric cruelty, and lack of true understanding of a God of unconditional love.

As we move towards the threshold of a new and more enlightened age, it should be put away, along with all unnecessary reminders of past ignorance, for it cannot be trusted in any way, for spiritual or any other form of guidance.

Chapter Three

Christianity: The Sad and Shameful Truth

It is possible to look at the history of Christianity and catalogue every conflict and war fought either in their name, or with their support and blessing. To list the atrocities, torture, maiming and deaths perpetrated, volumes could and have been written on such historical fact.

In this chapter I first mention just a few examples of the sad and shameful involvement of the Christian Church in past history. Then some accounts of how even in the twentieth century those in positions of authority from within the Church suppressed the truth of communication from those residing in the spirit realms after 'death.'

Additionally, how they blocked the truth about potential benefits obtainable through Spiritual healing. Consequently, they denied their own followers, simply because those in authority did not wish to disturb their ancient teachings which put faith ahead of peoples' right to the truth.

Finally, I include reference to the ongoing shameful misuse of power that has seemingly allowed the Catholic Christian Church to elevate themselves above the laws of the land and cover-up criminal acts by their priests.

But to begin with, the first wars I would like to remind readers of are the so called "Holy Wars" or "Crusades" which spanned nearly two hundred years, from 1095 to 1291. At this time religious fever was at its most destructive, for the Crusades resulted in the deaths of hundreds of thousands of men, women and children, all because of the intolerance and hatred the Christian popes and bishops had for the Turks for taking the lands which they deemed the birth place of Jesus from the Jewish people.

The first five of the official eight crusades were organised directly by the Pope (and his confederates), with most of the following information available in the Encyclopaedia Britannia. For the first crusade, Pope Urban II in 1095 called for a Christian army to recapture the "Holy Sepulchre" (which is a church within the walled Old City of Jerusalem), resulting in the capture of Jerusalem.

When in 1144 the state of Edessa, in Turkey (which was a "crusader state" established after the first crusade), fell again to the Muslim Turks, Pope Eugenius III called for the second crusade, which ended in failure. The Turkish leader Saladin and his army had by 1187 captured Jerusalem, with the result that Pope Gregory VIII called for the third crusade (1189-92). This was initially led by Emperor Frederick I of Germany, but he died a year later, and from then on was jointly led by Richard I, the 'Lion-heart' of England, and Phillip II Augustus of France.

Richard, on route, took Cyprus and joined Phillip II Augustus in the siege of Acre. After failing to reach Jerusalem, in 1192 Richard negotiated a five-year peace treaty with Saladin which permitted European pilgrims access to 'holy' shrines, and prepared to undertake his return journey.

To many people, the name of Richard I and the word "Crusades" conjures up images from the old Hollywood film, "Robin Hood," especially the sight of 'good' King Richard and his knights returning from the 'holy' lands with some wearing tunics emblazoned with a large cross. In the film the return of King Richard marks the end of the reign of terror, torture and tyranny which in his absence was inflicted on the people by his 'evil' brother John. It leads us to believe that Richard must have stood for all that was British, proud, noble and good. But how many people pause to consider the injustice of slaughtering Turkish men, women and children simply because of their different religious beliefs?

Religious intolerance and hatred was the true motive for the crusades; they had nothing to do with attempting to right the wrong of one race taking land from another, for in those days such acts were a regular occurrence. If the Turks had been Christian, and not Moslem, no crusade would have taken place.

Similarly, I wonder how many people have been taught that King Richard, at the Muslim garrison of Acre, had 2700 male prisoners killed, plus their wives and children, bringing the figure in some estimates to 4000, with the bodies being disembowelled in search of gold and silver, after he had found some flaw in the selection of prisoners returned to him in an exchange arrangement with the Turkish leader Saladin.

But this was apparently typical of King Richard, for it is reported that he argued and fell out with everyone - including Phillip II Augustus. After a brief return to England, he then waged war upon Phillip in Normandy for five years. Richard eventually died from wounds received during a siege upon a castle at Chalus, at 42 years of age. During his reign as King from 1189-1199, Richard spent less than one year in England, such was his love of warfare.

I conclude that those who led the Crusades, including King Richard, behaved no better towards their enemies, classified as such by their religion, than King John behaved in the film towards the people of Nottingham. We should all remember that apart from the knights and noblemen, the majority of the ordinary people were referred to, and treated as, peasants.

The Fourth Crusade was called by Pope Innocent III in 1198 against Constantinople (Istanbul) but perhaps the most shameful and sad crusade was the "Children's Crusade" (unofficially the fifth) of 1212, although some historians have attempted to divert papal blame and record that it was (somehow) led by a French boy named Stephen and a 10 year-old German boy named Nicholas.

For this crusade, fifty thousand children, boys and girls, were taken from France (30,000) and Germany (20,000) to take on the Moslems. The religious 'reasoning' behind this tragedy was a crazy belief that the other crusades must have failed because the men were too worldly and not pure enough for such a 'divine' mission.

The children of course did not stand a chance, and all but a few were lost through disease, drowning on route, actual conflict, and perhaps the least unfortunate ones, through capture and slavery. The fifth official Crusade of 1215 was again called for by Pope Innocent III, and this one ended with a truce.

Another famous and bloody period of history dominated by the Christian religion was the Spanish Inquisition, which was established with approval of the Pope by Ferdinand V and Isabella in 1479, and not suppressed until 1820. Ironically, much of Spain, which in those days was still divided into smaller kingdoms, was a predominantly Moslem country until the early part of the twelfth century when it was overran by the Christian armies. Although until 1492 some areas were still following the Moslem religion.

Invasion and forced religious conversion, to the Christian Church, was of course considered a justifiable act. If the people were not taught the history of Jesus, were not baptised, and did not believe wholeheartedly in him as the son of God, then they were considered doomed to hell anyway. So invading any country in the name of Christianity was considered a duty (in reality this was a sad and shameful excuse).

But for Spain, as with many other countries who are now staunchly Christian, how the centuries changed them. Before the invasion of the Christian armies, the Spanish were highly cultured, and progressive in their education, medicine, and agriculture, with public baths, parks, markets and mosques all reportedly superior to those of Christian Europe. Education and the cultural benefits this can bring were considered undesirable by the zealous Christian Church.

In time, Spain played a major role in the race to convert the world to Christianity (using inquisitional torture), while at the same time becoming richer through looting and taking whatever they fancied to add to their wealth from those countries they conquered (as did the British Empire).

This despicable period of religious intolerance used methods of torture such as the rack, thumb screws, the burning out of eyes, hot irons to melt flesh and muscle, crucifixion and burning at the stake, and many more cruel and degrading methods to convert people to Christianity, and to punish and kill all those who refused.

The religious conversion of the cultures invaded was not enough to satisfy the soldiers who made up these armies; they had to be paid and kept for their services. The spoils of war (whatever the state had not taken) were theirs, and when the rewards were not great enough to justify the expenditure, other ways were found to make profit.

One of these was the slave trade, which went on with the full approval of the Christian bishops and ministers. To justify the slave trade, the bishops once again quoted from Leviticus, where it confirms that to 'take bondmen or bondmaids, and to buy and sell them as possessions,' is perfectly acceptable. The slaves are referred to as heathen, which actually meant those of other races or religions.

Not content with permitting the slave trade to operate for hundreds of years, many ministers held stock in the enterprise (as did many nobles, including Queen Elizabeth I of England), and this continued until the nineteenth century.

The fact that other passages from the Bible could be interpreted against slavery was never given any consideration by the Church, as always, their own self interest came before truth and justice. The enormity of the slave trade, and the part played by the British can be gathered by the fact that a fleet of 192 British ships with capacity for over 47,000 slaves was engaged in the eighteenth century.

The African slave trade, with many taken to America, operated from 1510 until late in the 19th century, and estimates as to the number of slaves taken run as high as 20 million. Many did not survive the Atlantic passage. They were chained, beaten, and near-starved with no sanitation; if they died they were thrown overboard, and if the ship sank they remained shackled and doomed to a watery grave.

The power of the Christian bishops and ministers, and their effect upon the entire world, has been profound. They never let the light of reason or truth stand in their way, and whenever anyone took a stand which did not meet with their approval, they condemned and branded the individual as evil and in league with the devil. Such was their power, that torture and death was the likely consequence facing anyone who dared to speak out against them.

Such a fate was inevitable for mediums (and healers, herbalists etc) and basically anyone who opposed the Church in the slightest. Mediums were given the title of witches, and branded evil and in league with the devil. Torture, to confess association with the devil, was inevitable for all mediums who dared to deny the absurd lie, followed by death by drowning, or being burned alive at the stake.

The number of mediums disposed of in this manner ran into thousands, not only in Britain, but throughout the Christian world. The last medium, or witch as she was referred to, was burned in England as recently as 1712. Torture was also used as a method of extracting confessions in cases of believed witchcraft. In 1252 Pope Innocent IV authorised its use.

By the fourteenth century it was in general use in the tribunals of the Inquisition, and it was particularly used in cases of (supposed) witchcraft where evidence was difficult to find. In 1468 the Pope removed all legal limits on the application of torture in such cases.

Tortures used include: crushing the tips of fingers and toes in a vice; a rack which violently stretched the body; the "Leg-screw" or "Spanish boot" which squeezed the calf and broke the shin-bone in pieces (described as 'the most severe and cruel pain in the world'); the "Ram" or "Witch-chair," a seat of spikes, heated from below; or to have one's finger-nails pulled off with pincers or needles driven up, and many, many more.

When a so-called Witch confessed (in an attempt to stop the pain), the next stage was to secure from her, again under torture, a list of all those of her neighbours whom she had recognised at the "Witches' Sabbath" (a meeting). Then a fresh set of trials and tortures would begin.

God knows how many hundreds of thousands had been murdered before the close of this barbarous era in history based on the often quoted passage in the Old Testament from Exodus 'You should not allow a witch to live,' a passage which was clearly entered by ancient priests to dispose of all those who could teach the truth and expose their lies (such an entry is not to be found in any of the early manuscripts).

The lies, intolerance and murderous actions of those proclaiming the Christian faith since its inception, according some historians, has resulted in the deaths of a minimum of twenty-five million people.

The absurd power and influence of the Christian Church was such that in Britain, until the middle of the nineteenth century, the simple act of not believing in the teachings of Christianity was enough to have a person imprisoned. Even in America two hundred years ago things were not much better. One of the pioneers of the laws of liberty, of which all are so proud, Thomas Paine (1737-1809), produced a book called "The Age of Reason." In his book he dared to suggest that Jesus was not God, and that the Old Testament was too barbarous to be the word of God.

Something all sensible freethinking people would these days agree with. But in his day, Thomas Paine was denounced and cursed by Christian ministers, and was never again allowed true liberty, and it became dangerous for him to be seen in public.

Thomas Paine was born in Norfolk (UK) on 29 January 1737, but in a class controlled system he failed to make much of a life for himself, so he immigrated to America, and at the age of thirty-seven, found his true spiritual home. His talents were quickly recognised, and he became a pioneer of free-thought, and was first to speak and write in favour of the rights of independence for all people, and for the abolition of slavery. His writings resulted in the first American anti-slavery society being formed in Philadelphia. He was also a pioneer in pleading the rights of women, and even for fair treatment for the animal kingdom.

He was a brave man, and even dared to speak out against the immoral existence of a British monarchy, a family adored by so many, who owe their position, status and wealth to the barbaric domination of their ancestors. If only such a person as Thomas Paine could have lived and guided us through each generation, the world would be a far better place to live in today.

To give readers a better understanding of Thomas Paine, I have paraphrased together a few passages from his book. They also demonstrate his bravery, for it was written and published around 1795.

'All national institutions of Churches, whether Jewish, Christian, or Turkish, appear to me no other than human inventions set up to terrify, enslave, and monopolize power and profit.

'Whenever we read the obscene stories, the voluptuous debaucheries, the cruel and torturous executions, the unrelenting vindictiveness with which more than half the Bible is filled, it would be more consistent that we called it the word of a demon than the word of God. It is a history of wickedness, that has served to corrupt and brutalise and, for my own part, I sincerely detest it, as I detest everything that is cruel.

'As to the Christian system of faith, it introduces between man and his Maker an opaque body which it calls a redeemer; as the moon introduces her opaque self between the earth and the sun, and it produces by this means a religious or an irreligious eclipse of light. It has put the whole orbit of reason into shade.'

Thomas Paine was so far ahead of his time that even today many people have still not reached his level of understanding. As for 'the age of reason' it is now dawning and the new light that it brings is gradually enlightening the world.

It would seem very unfair to blame the teachings of Christianity for the atrocities carried out against the Jewish people during the Second World War. Yet in his book "Mein Kampf" (meaning "My Struggle") Adolf Hitler said that he was 'acting in accordance with the will of God, because, in defending myself against the Jews, I am fighting to defend the work of Christ.' He also said that 'the greatness of Christianity lay not in any effort to reconcile itself with the philosophies of the ancients, which had some likeness with its own, but in the unrelenting and bigoted expounding and defending of its own doctrines.'

Arthur Findlay, in his epic book "The Curse of Ignorance" said that 'Christian principles, Christian ideals, Christian culture, and the Christian way of life stand for everything wicked and reactionary to everyone who knows past history, and only those who do not know, or do not think, will ever use this word to describe something good, just and kind.'

So far in this chapter I have mainly dealt with some of the historical aspects of Christianity, which thankfully have mainly been curtailed by more sensible laws. But there are other aspects which are just as important; these are the acts of suppression of spiritual truth by the Christian Church, which have affected the lives of countless millions of people upon this planet. To deliberately ignore truth and keep their flocks in ignorance has been a cowardly act of shameful 'self-preservation' by the Church.

In 1938 the Church of England was presented with the opportunity to change their standpoint, to bring their religion forward to a new era, but they declined to do so.

It was the year in which a report was handed to the Archbishop of Canterbury, the results of an investigation which the Church itself had commissioned into Spiritualism and its survival evidence.

Much work would have been required to bring about a new form of Christianity, one which could have accepted Jesus as a spiritual master, teacher and healer, but the Archbishop of Canterbury and the Church of England failed to take the steps necessary to bring about such a revolution of free-thought.

This, despite the fact that their report found favour with Spiritualism, with a majority of seven to three confirming spirit world communication and cooperation as factual. But alas the Church of England refused to publicly publish its own majority report.

However, someone with integrity within the Christian Church must have been feeling guilty, for a copy of the report was eventually sent to the "Psychic News" (now a monthly magazine) in London during late 1947. So nine years were wasted before the report was finally available to the public. But with very few Christians reading the Psychic News, and no official support from the

Church of England, or change in their approach, sermons and teaching, they might just as well have not bothered with any investigation in the first place.

The Church of England select committee included the Bishop of Bath and Wells, the Dean of St. Paul's, the Master of the Temple, a professor of the Christian religion at Oxford University, and other notable persons. Their report was never acted upon because the Archbishops, namely of Canterbury and York, preferred to keep Christians ignorant of the truth.

The following are some paraphrased extracts from the report.

'It is claimed by Spiritualists that the character of many events as recorded in the Gospels, is precisely that of psychic phenomena, and that the evidence for the paranormal occurrences which Spiritualism has adduced strongly confirms the historicity of the Gospel records, in the sense that they also are records of paranormal occurrences, including instances for example, of clairvoyance (in the story of Nathaniel) and of materialization (in the feeding of the five thousand, and above all in the narrative of the Resurrection appearances).

'The miracles of healing are acclaimed as closely parallel to the healings performed through mediums. It is strongly urged that if we do not accept the evidence for modern psychical happenings, we should not, apart from long tradition, accept the Gospel records either. It is certainly true that there are quite clear parallels between the miraculous events recorded in the Gospel and modern phenomena attested by Spiritualists. And if we assert that the latter must be doubted because they have not yet proved capable of scientific statement and verification, we must add that the miracles, and the Resurrection itself, are not capable of such verification either. We must therefore ask what the proper Christian grounds of belief in these central truths of Christianity are. The answer to this question is clearly that we believe upon a basis of faith, and not of demonstrable scientific knowledge.

'We do not accept the Gospels because they record wonders, but because they ring true to the deepest powers of spiritual apprehension which we possess. But if this is so, we must clearly apply similar criteria to the claims of Spiritualists, and this means that while we regard some part of these claims as matter proper to the scientist, we regard some other parts of these claims as not properly capable of scientific verification or dispute, but, at the same time, as deserving the consideration of Christians upon grounds of another kind. We think that it is probable that the hypothesis that they (the communications) proceed in some cases from discarnate spirits is the true one. There is no reason why we should not accept gladly the assurance that we are still in closest contact with those who have been dear to us in this life, who are going forward. It is, in our opinion, important that representatives of the Church should keep in touch with groups of intelligent persons who believe in Spiritualism.'

How different Christians of today might have been if this report had ever been officially released to the public and acted upon.

A similar fate (to be ignored) awaited another investigation the Church of England undertook. In 1951 the Archbishops of Canterbury and York decided to appoint a committee to investigate "Spiritual healing," or "Divine healing" as they chose to call it. It took the Archbishops over two years, until October 1953, to simply appoint a committee, which was made up of some twenty-two people, including eleven of their own ministers, of which five were bishops, and also eight people from the medical profession.

It took another five years, until June 1958, before the report was finally published, and what a waste of paper it proved to be. It totally ignored conclusive evidence presented by Harry Edwards (the greatest spiritual healer of his day) and even failed to acknowledge that spiritual healing could have any beneficial results. Most of the evidence was in the form of proven case histories.

Harry Edwards was allowed to personally address the commission for fifteen minutes, during which time he explained how he defined the term "Spiritual healing," and how he considered it divine, in the sense of it being channelled healing, coming from a higher source than himself. He also presented the commission with over seventy documented case histories for them to examine and verify at their convenience, despite the fact they asked for, and would have been content with, just six cases. Many of the seventy plus individuals had been given up by their own doctors as incurable; all of them had responded well to the spiritual healing channelled through Harry Edwards, with many cures being hailed as miracles by the patients' own doctors, since the cases had been considered incurable.

One might have expected some positive interest to have been shown, especially amongst the doctors and other medical people on the commission, with their interest in saving lives and healing the sick. Yet ludicrously one of the doctors suggested that all seventy plus cases could have been instances of spontaneous healing, and after making this absurd statement, the doctor in question literally turned his back on Harry Edwards, and refused to acknowledge any of his evidence. This, despite the fact that the patients' own doctors could have confirmed the results obtained through spiritual healing, but the commission had not even asked them to give evidence.

The reaction of this doctor was typical of the orthodox medical authority in those days, with any evidence of spiritual healing being explained away as mislabelled x-rays, spontaneous healing or remission, mistaken diagnosis, medical inefficiency, temporary response through suggestion, and many other such comments, which if all true, would have made a mockery of the medical profession's competence. For, if all or even the majority of cases presented by Harry Edwards were diagnostic errors made by the medical profession, it would have meant that errors were occurring in colossal numbers.

Shamefully, even before the commission members had all finally been appointed, the Archbishop of York, during 1952, had set the tone, and pre-empted the thinking of his bishops and other ministers, by stating that cures obtained through spiritual healing were not permanent. Under these conditions, it would have been an act of defiance, no doubt with repercussions, for any of his staff if they had reached other than the same conclusion.

When the Church commission finally published its report into spiritual healing in 1958, not one of the seventy plus cases had been investigated, and not one patient was ever interviewed or examined by the commission, and none of the patients' own doctors were asked for their case records.

Harry Edwards also offered to allow those on the commission to attend as many healing sessions as they wished, to see for themselves how he practiced his healing, and the results which could be forthcoming, but nobody on the commission took up the offer. The medical profession and the Church had linked forces, and buried their heads in the sand, completely ignoring all the evidence, and the opportunity to verify the validity of spiritual healing.

The report finally made suggestions such as that 'doctors and churchmen should unite to exorcise demons and evil spirits' from patients; statements which amount to no more than a perpetuation of their Dark Age ideas on the causes of ill health. They also said that any priest called to attend a sick person should first make sure the patient was a baptised Christian before any help could be offered. Furthermore, the patient should be prepared to confess sins and take communion before any healing was to be attempted, which would also not be possible until the priest had received a medical diagnosis. If all priests undertake such actions before they can even pray for a sick person, many patients would probably pass while waiting. Finally, when the priest is ready (if the patient is still alive), the whole Christian procedure is one of ritual, with gestures to be performed and set words spoken.

The evidence which Harry Edwards supplied to the commission was irrefutable; and hundreds of doctors and many ministers of the Church privately wrote to confirm their belief in spiritual healing. Finally, in 1977 the General Medical Council of Britain accepted that Spiritual healing could in certain cases be beneficial.

For how many more years can Christian authorities ignore the overwhelming evidence of continuous life, and hide behind their inherited past, shamefully suppressing and denying the right of truth to the many millions of Christians the world over?

Finally today, the early years of the twenty-first century, when most decent people would think that none can openly defy the laws of the land in any so-called civilised country, we find that the Catholic Christian Church seem able to do so.

Only recently the United Nations (UN) children's rights experts condemned the Church for allowing clerical abuse – Priests who were or still are paedophile predators - to go on unchecked for decades. They also criticised them (to say the least) for their continued refusal to admit the extent of the problem, and their failure to adopt adequate measures to prevent further crimes, as they kept their 'code of silence.'

The investigators estimate that tens of thousands of children worldwide have been sexually abused by clerics.

According to the UN report 'well-known child sex abusers' were for years 'being transferred from parish to parish in an attempt to cover their crimes.' As a result of moving rather than reporting paedophiles - in many countries – dozens of child sex offenders are reported to still be in contact with children. The Vatican has confirmed that between 2008 and 2012 almost 400 priests had been "defrocked" for assaulting children.

The Catholic Church regarded (and perhaps still do) themselves above the law - that it was or still is their right to 'prosecute' their own priests. The maximum punishment they inflict is to defrock, in other words "dismiss" - historically without necessarily reporting the case to the police. To put it another way, and to repeat, "they shamefully covered-up" and are so guilty that they have paid out literally billions of dollars in settlements of compensation claims. In one joint claim alone, involving 508 cases, the Los Angeles Archdiocese paid a record-breaking $660 million (£324 million).

This is the sad and shameful truth.

Chapter Four

The Way Forward

It is a certainty that many Christian ministers have a greater understanding of the true spiritual nature of life than they are permitted, or permit themselves, to teach from their rostrums. But surely the first responsibility of any teacher, whether of religion or any other subject, is to teach the truth, no matter whether it offends those who do not wish to hear it, or those who would wish to deny it.

Those in positions of authority within the Church will no doubt fear ridicule for their past history and more recent cover-ups. Yet if they were to open their hearts to the truth, they would find that truth, and not falsehood, is really the only foundation worth building upon.

Spirit world communication and co-operation will not destroy people's faith in God. The messages of love those from the spirit world bring uplift and inspire people to live a more spiritual life. Surely this is something that should be welcomed by everyone claiming to work for God.

Formalised worship in churches serves no purpose other than as a gathering of like-minded individuals.

We worship God by living a good life – by caring, sharing, and developing a forgiving nature towards each other. I believe Silver Birch said that "service" is worship to God.

There are many good people the world over who call themselves "Christian." Typically they go to their local churches and enjoy the social side that is often on offer while never thinking too much about past history – or even worrying too much about the offences of individuals within the churches. The past cannot be changed, but the future can.

One step would be to acknowledge that mediumship should never have been condemned by the Church or within the Bible. Another would be to open their doors so that mediumship can be reintroduced in all Christian Churches.

Genuine mediums are able to relay reassuring and loving messages from those who have simply moved-on to a higher level of expression. There is nothing to fear in demonstrations of mediumship. Fear was created by the ancient clergy because of their greed and self-interest.

Furthermore, higher spirit communicators are able to relay information about every aspect of what most people would call the afterlife. Indeed, many books have already been written.

Therefore, my advice is to go forward with an open mind and, if you haven't already done so, investigate fully for yourself, and I am confident in saying that what you will find is that everything herein is the truth.

Everlasting life is guaranteed to all – no religion is required.

What we call God is the Power and Source, the eternal consciousness, expressed within all life.

Recommended Reading

I mention just a few books below; you will find many more listed at my website.

If you seek further proof of the spiritual nature of life including scientific research and discoveries, near-death experiences, and much more, then I suggest reading:

A Lawyer Presents the Evidence for the Afterlife
By Victor and Wendy Zammit

If you would like more information on the history of religion or the Bible Old Testament then read:

The Rock of Truth by Arthur Findlay
When Prophets Spoke (Spiritualism in the Old Testament) by Rev. G. Maurice Elliott

Some of the most informative spirit teaching books, channelled by Robert Goodwin, contain the teachings of White Feather, these include:

Truth from the White Brotherhood; The Golden Thread; Answers for an Enquiring Mind; In the Presence of White Feather; The Enlightened Soul; Wisdom of White Feather

Two books I find most interesting as well as informative contain deep hypnosis case studies of life between lives by Michael Newton, they are:

Journey of Souls
Destiny of Souls

Made in the USA
Charleston, SC
23 April 2014